The Moor of The Bronx

poems by

Ricardo Nazario y Colón

Finishing Line Press
Georgetown, Kentucky

The Moor of The Bronx

Copyright © 2023 by Ricardo Nazario y Colón
ISBN 979-8-88838-224-0 First Edition
All rights reserved under International and Pan-American Copyright Conventions. No part of this book may be reproduced in any manner whatsoever without written permission from the publisher, except in the case of brief quotations embodied in critical articles and reviews.

ACKNOWLEDGMENTS

I am grateful to the editors of these publications for giving my work a home.

"Elemental," The Single Hound, December 2011; "El Perfumar," The Single Hound, December 2011; "Green Space," Acentos Review, November 2010; "Papo Hueso," Blood Lotus Journal, 2012; "Ghetto Life," Pluck! The Journal of Affrilachian Arts & Culture Issue #6, 2012; " Salt In the Wind," The Round Table, 2011; "Magic Box," The Round Table 2011; "Wild Fig Trees," Aphros Review, 2011; "Annabel Lee and Me," Tidal Basin Review, 2012; "Bacalao," Broken Circles Anthology, Cave Moon Press 2011; "Chocolate Cake," Broken Circles Anthology, Cave Moon Press 2011; "The Moor of The Bronx," Tidal Basin Review, 2012; "Preguntas," Nashville's Poetry in Motion, 2012.

With gratitude to
The Affrilachian Poets, Megan Pillow, Tracy Bonilla, Holler Poetry Series, Jane Curan, The North Carolina Poetry Society, Gilbert-Chappell Mentor Series, Teneice Durrant, Western Carolina University Spring Festival, and the Greensboro Book Festival.

Publisher: Leah Huete de Maines
Editor: Christen Kincaid
Cover Art: upfromsumdirt / Ronald Davis
Author Photo: Ashley T. Evans
Cover Design: Elizabeth Maines McCleavy

Order online: www.finishinglinepress.com
also available on amazon.com

Author inquiries and mail orders:
Finishing Line Press
P. O. Box 1626
Georgetown, Kentucky 40324
U. S. A.

Table of Contents

Jíbaro

El Perfumar 1

Elemental 3

Morivivi 4

Origin of NEGRITO 5

Pésame 6

Ajo 7

Lechusa 8

Keeping Memories 9

El Vocero, 1968 10

Escalofrío 11

The Devil's Triangle 12

Making Dough 13

Benevolent Assimilation 14

The Bloodletting of Salt and Chlorine 15

And I will follow 17

Larry Davis

Green Space 21

Saturday at Mullaly Park 22

Black & Bruise 23

Making a Stool Pigeon 24

Festival of Heroes 25

Johnny on the Pony 26

Bogus Realty Company 1 27

Weapons Count 29

Operation Condor 30

Loco Larry 32

Bogus Realty Company 2 34

Charges 35

Bonfire of the Vanities 36

Robo Cop 37

Yes, Lord 39

Thursday 7:00 PM 40

El South Bronx

The Moor of The Bronx 43

The Crease of Almidón 44

Angels on the Corner 45

Annabel Lee and Me 46

Autumn in the Bronx 47

Tap Out 48

The Other Side of Plexiglas 49

Window Washers 50

No Obituary 51

Safe en Casa 52

Hambre 54

El Building 56

If They See Us 57

Concentric Days 59

Fuego 60

Papo Hueso 62

Jíbaro

This term has multiple connotations; the rural identity of a Puerto Rican; it has also been used to represent the negative aspect of a community but overall it is a point of identity pride for Puerto Ricans in the diaspora.

El Perfumar

for Kate Andry

In la plaza
old men cut in hats and guayaberas
sing the morning wake.

They hold memories of Jíbaros
on carretas, full of papas and ajos.
Café steams on their lips.

Su perfumar conjures smiles,
for men's hearts beat like marble.
She is Yemaya
making water of them
who sit—sweat on their brow,
wilted muscles like forgotten
cemetery flowers.

Traces of cobalt in their eyes
hold secrets behind retina clouds of grey.
This one—used to climb palm trees
with limbs curved
by the saddle of a horse.

Her touch, soft on sea air skin
makes them muse; bodies hunger
to become young again.
They recall the songs of patchouli
shimmering, the rocking of leaves
descending to the ground.

Today's sun, not yet awake
slows time to read
news of absent stories.
There are no women in the lives
of these men, no one to rearrange
their insides.

Only their broad voices
dark purple harmonize songs,
keeping the old ways alive in them;
guarding her night.

Elemental

Who made the ten-string guitar, El Cuatro?
Who gave Puerto Rican women hips and the men Paso Fino?
Who made the Bolero? You know—
a dance that cannot be described by just any word.
Too intimate and simple. It makes grownups unfaithful.

Tell me how his feet brought her off the chair.
How her breast was teenage breathing when their hands touched.
Tell me again, he was the devil—that his brimstone did not
smell of custard apples and mangos. Show me his burnt mark—
his calling card still remained when she was entombed.

Morivivi

Para la prima Judith Ortiz-Cofer

En la loma del viento where we imagined
pyramids with tails catching wind, while
sailing diurnally across the sky, there,
you taught my bare feet, the price of
waking the *Morivivi*.

In *Hormigueros*, when you were
a little girl, the grown ups told you

> *"las niñas no saltan sobre
> alambres de púas"*

nor do they play with cow pies.
Your dress sometimes snagged
at the further most *guardarraya*,
en resistencia.

One the day you disappeared
I found your note *entre las hojas
dormidas. Tus palabras* leaving
for a foreign time, *decian,*
    Para el primo,
    *Me voy afuera, busca por mi
    adentro del sol.*
Today, the familiar warmth,
me despierta
        como el toque
                al Morivivi.

Origin of NEGRITO

First Known Use: On the 6th day of creation.

ne·gri·to /nəˈgrētō/

—noun
1.
Of sweet as fruit, like the Blue Grape, Black Berry, Chocolate Pudding Fruit, Cherokee Purple, Chocolate Cherry, Berkely Tie Dye, Black Brandywine, Black Krim, Black Pineapple, Black Plum, Black Sea Man, Black Zebra, Brown Berry, Carbon, Cherokee Chocolate, Indian Stripe, Indische Fliesh, Japanese Black Triefele, Paul Robeson, Purple Calabash, Purple Pear Brandywine, Purple Russian, Southern Night, Violet Jasper, Zebra Cherry Hybrid, Shawnee, Navaho, Chactow, Cheyenne, Comanche, Smooth Stem, Thornless, Glossy, Shine, Ebony, and Satin.

2.
The last state of sweetness, like a Black Skin Banana, Avocado, Plantain, Olive.

3.
of, pertaining to, or characteristic of Love, Like, Adore.

4.
of, Pilar Barbosa, Celia Cruz, La Lupe, Antonia Pantoja, Edwige Danticat, Mamá Tíngo, Samaná Americans, Alejo Beni, Toña La Negra, Lucy "La Muñeca de Chocolate" Fabery, Isabel "La Negra" Luberza Oppenheimer, Carlitos Colón, Ismael Rivera, Mongo Santamaría, Patato Valdez, Bizcocho, Don Pedro Albizu Campos, Nicolás Guillén, Rafael Cordero, Roberto Clemente Walker, Teofilio Stephenson, y Sammy Davis Jr.

Pésame

for Facundo Colón

If I could, I would ask Agüelo about the day—
what he was doing when he heard the sound,
what he felt the night after Nereida died.

I would hug him and say
"Agüelo, te vi con la palanca,"
en batalla contra columbras de casa,
El barrio, en estado de horror.

If I could, I would wipe the tears streaming
from his yellow eyes and let the sun dry
the rest of his clay and sweet sugarcane face.

It would be the only time that he and I touch.

Ajo

Rare was the town in Puerto Rico
without a Plaza.
Uncle Colón sold ajos from una
esquina de la nueva a la vieja.
La carreta filled almost always
pulled by an old Spaniard's horse.
He remembered them after they lost
the war to iron ships.
In groups of twelves, they marched,
como huevos.
Their eyes strike his like wrought iron,
striked a lower price.
Among themselves, they talked
like horses behind barb-wire fences.
Bulbs dangled before these soldiers
who no longer saw themselves
as kindred.
He sold them ajos.

Lechuza

Jostle and manhandle, there are no roads to lull us to sleep.
No curves that blind or heart thump ravines. No tree branches
low, bursting with fruit and I am wedged
in the passenger cabin between mother and brother.
I stare for the first time at the red buckle of your seatbelt sign.

Our road—transparent, tasteless, made of molecules,
makes sense of the steepness of *Flores* hill, the fallen *aguacates*,
and the fireflies along the cemetery's path.
The rear tires are clean and tucked away, the way women
of the time hid knotted-up handkerchiefs in their bosom.
The Audubon of orange and yellow; a canvas for the
lies somewhere in the sky three hours ago—
and here we are—back in New York.with its old skyscrapers,
bustling streets, and strange tongues. Gone are the *cabritos,
cercas de alambres, mosquitos, y la calma del coqui.*

From JFK airport to the South Bronx, I stare at the moon,
ripe as honeydew. I ask again for time,
for her shadow to spread her *Lechuza* wings.

Keeping Memories

for Clotilde Colón López

Everything begins with the memory
caras en pañuelos trekking—of agile legs
finding footing like the goats they tend.

I keep the time of these memories;
of the old Eben-Ezer church on cemetery hill;
of Evangelism spreading its *Lechusa* wings.

Carruzos with its last name neighborhoods—
Figueroas on one arm, *Flores* on the other;
the river flows around *como capa* to the *López's*.

Another old-timer flies *en este invierno ardiente.*
People burst like ripe fruit during windstorms.
A través de tiempos *abuela* was dearly loved.

Ants hold on to grass blades, protecting
kin from the coming flood. It rains inside
this small town, especially on searing days.

El Vocero, 1968

Under the bureaus' glass top,
among the pictures of family
and friends only known to her, an article—

my mother at nineteen
smiling in her wedding gown
standing next to him—
a name I have tried hard to forget.

I imagine the chaos in my uncle's house—
the one she ran away from
to marry the other half of the story.

Single mother of three boys,
returns to *cuero, sucia, mal criada*
and the finger-pointing esas.

Forty-three years of tending skillets
for fatherless boys should have produced
a steel riveted heart,

but to his death bed, we came.
Unsure of our footing
yet proud to represent her,
even if the mayfly lived longer
than his interest.

Escalofrío

for Martín Colón and Milagros Colón

I visited a nursing home today. Spent time with a patient,
dying. Saw fingernail bites on his skin.
Made me think of you. By your wrist, strapped to the bed
like you were some kind of mass-murderer.

I wrote a letter to this person. He says to me "I love you,"
I ask whom, he fades out as he whispers "time."

I write.

My pocket spiral reads, "I love you time!" I punctuate
with an exclamation. The nurse tells me the morphine
keeps him adrift. I wait, drawn to his love of time.

I'm curious why there are no medicines in his room.
It comes to me; this is not a real nursing home.

Are there just four destinations in this Grand Central Station?
Heaven, hell, purgatory, oblivion; I see no bible,
no Koran, no Virgen de Guadalupe, no Santa Barbara candle.

Just the clear drip of morphine wanes its way into him.
I cannot tell if his skin is chilled like mud. I want
to embrace you, but the latex robs me of your touch, time
robs me, geography robs me, and I cannot weep for you.

The nurse tells me he is not going to wake up. I ask—
she tells me it is not easy. I grab his hand—it is warm
like smoke. I wrap my fist and put his hand in my pocket.

I don't want him to go the way you did, without seeing
a smile, without feeling the warmth and suppleness of my hands.

The Devil's Triangle

rum sent to africa
africans made slaves
slaves brought
to the west indies
to farm sugar cane
to make molasses
to sell to america
to make the rum
to send to africa
to trade for
africans

Making Dough

for Roberto Nazario

In the slur of his words, a gap, left by the missing murmur of his heart. My Robert was too old for me to know, the way one should know a big brother. Aware of the volatility in our lives, he taught me how to play with the loot from his high school's chess club. He doesn't know I hold this family heirloom in my hand the way pleaded skin presses on plastic covers in the memory of our Bronx living room.

I hold his words cupped: An ice cream cone on McClellan Street soothed the scabs and calluses as he guided me away to paper filled offices and suits. Inside the latrine, between the tin walls and a nameless piece of pine or birch, a Maria Juana filled matchbox. I, like Judas, sold my brother's solace for the prize of a glance at Pilate's sister's underwear.

The first man I kissed--his stubble beard aged long before my eyes cast themselves on him. He tried to pull away in a panic. The second time he warned me with a gesture. I told him I loved him. His shuriken fingers wrapped around my shoulder blades and my lips pressed on his cheek—we were both disarmed.

We inherited no traditions on how to love. No father to model how to hold hands when it rains at funerals. We just kneaded with the heel of our palms, always pushed forward, and folded into one another—clean, pressed and sometimes with wrinkles, until we pinched.

Benevolent Assimilation

Or let me crap in your mouth, President William McKinley

I was born *Gringo* in the South Bronx,
in between the Third Avenue L and Alexander's

A long time ago, a *Tecato* was gonna dissect
mami's belly full of Oscar until God intervened.

Puerto Rico mi Isla del Encato my first memory
of you is in a sun-faded Polaroid photograph I keep.

We produce nothing but revolutionaries, sell outs
and everyone caught in the struggles of Cain and Abel.

How many generations of Dick and Jane will
it take to erase a culture anchored in old

conquistadores? Who now are bilingual *hablando Español
e Ingles*, in front of nations united in modern slavery.

For a deportation President whose darkens the planet
the way eagle wings cast a shadow on seven continents.

McKinley, the oldest colony in the world, cries out
your name. A spectre behind a Hollywood sign that read

Si Se Puede rewrote itself to the White House.
In benevolent assimilation inside the west wing

ovules echo an undetermined people; *mi gente
de mas alla* are drunk like empty barrels of rum

washed on the shores of *Guanica*, a sanctified place,
where *los murmullos* of patriots speak the words

of freedom: yes, we can.

The Bloodletting of Salt and Chlorine

He'd never said if you father a child
Make sure you are around to raise him.

Then I'd think how could he not speak
to the younger version of me. Afraid of shadows.

Of course, he could not speak in his absence
but mami spoke to him in Polaroid hieroglyphics.

Six memories imprinted within me like the
thirty year old tattoos I've carried on my flesh.

I was young. Less introspective and fearless
of time. Once, when I was in the military,

I watched a Marine fall from the sky. I bed
this memory of death every night. He was not

there to teach me right from wrong. Drunk
I stumbled through my youth. Life has not

been cruel, just practical. Like a kitchen knife
cuts through flesh, separating muscle fiber

from bone. In one smooth motion, I learned
how to still the blade. When I was a child

his hands never washed my hair, never felt

the pain of his nails rooting my thick curls.
His lips, a cloudy night sky, failed to form

constellation words of love for my ears
to listen to; my mother never fell below

the grown, although on some days she dust
him off from where he still lingered in her

bursting heart. She never drowned under
the rush of water that streaked across

her face; she still knew the difference between
the bloodletting of salt and chlorine.

And I will follow

I never asked
if he held me at birth.
If the twelve pounds I carried
were a measurable gift to him.
If he kissed me on the forehead
or held me close to his breast.
If his piano stained fingers
edged my newborn exterior.

Did he smile like men of his time,
half crooked and belly full?
Were they Cohibas or Montecristos?
Did he wire news overseas?

...El bebe is varon, stop
...Pesa 12 libras, stop
...No te preocupes, stop
...Este salió blanco, stop

Did he carry your luggage
when you boarded PanAm?

How are these answers
going to make him my father?

Larry Davis

Many people are familiar with Larry Davis and his notorious story. I knew Larry as just another guy who played street football with us.

Green Space

a larry davis story

Underneath the shadow
of the elevated 4 train.
In between Yankee stadium
and 167th street.
On any given Sunday,
Mullaly Park was filled
with syncopated conga sounds,
the intoxication of marijuana
and birds perched on trees
like low-hanging fruit.
It was a barge
of empty malt liquor bottles;
a Batey for worshipers
of forbidden African tongues.
A sanctuary for drug
Addicts and alcoholics;
a home for Christians
living in corrugated cardboard.
An underground railroad
for pigeons, seeking freedom
from tenement cages.

Saturday at Mullaly Park

a larry davis Story

I took a moon pie and a Malta from his hand.
He was slow on the adjustments but we needed a tenth.
Rare were the games he finished. Always on a mission,
with shapeshifting lechuza eyes. Looking beyond the fence.
An interception spiraled, and we had to explain—two hands.
He was high but not zooted, when the offense scored.
We took a walk to help him search for his pistol.
It always slipped through his denim jean wall.

Black & Bruise

a larry davis Story

In our neighborhood
we played many games,
in daylight and under
the watchful eye
of street lamps.
We had parks
long lost to muggers;
all given up
even the night.
We played Ringolevio,
Manhunt and Roundup.
Games played one way
don't get caught.
We were chased
como Toño Bicicleta
y Correa Cotto.
Felt the wind of machetes
and bullets yell our names
in the morning darkness.
There were no rules
for pastimes that began
after midnight.
Getting caught meant
being broken by punches.
A black & bruise
tattooed on our shoulders.
Another mark of a loser's life.
Body scars marking time.
A memoir few will read.

Making a Stool Pigeon

a larry davis Story

Across the street La Jara.
Unbuckles and bluckles
each minute inside their cars.
A bed of corpse flowers
focused on pollinators.

Dealers and hustlers man up
in a hurry: Nickel bags,
Dime bags, I don't handle
Cash! Go around the corner!

Day and night police stake
their prey like Tsavo lions. Bodies
stir in apprehension when the
wind blows.

On a rooftop near his stash, Larry
is cornered. There are always
Choices for the outcast, cooperate or
be judged and juried by Smith and
Wesson; suffer an unfortunate footing
accident; risk being known on the
street as a stoolie.

There are witnesses to this
event, they too are
pigeons in cages.

Festival of Heroes

a larry davis Story

La jara lives in Nanuet, Massapequa, and
other places with aboriginal names.

Spaces with green grass, minivans, and
car pools for children in soccer leagues.

On the day of his birth, old neighborhood
gangs screamed bullets in his hospital.

His crib was lined in-between two
dressers and a prayer against cannonballs.

La jara used pigeons to feed his
appetite, before the festival of heroes.

Johnny on the Pony

a larry davis story

The Zodiac bar was a refuge,
a detox center if you toiled
with the forgotten—
a place to discover numbness.
On winter's eve, at the witching
hour of hops and barley,
a traditional ritual took place
on the streets and sidewalks
of the Bronx. Intoxicated men
recalled memories of childhood
Games. They curse at each other—
stopped one mother short of a rumble.
At risk, neighborhood bragging rights
that did not exist for these outsiders.
Which Force was better
at Johnny on the Pony?

An intense game added blood,
skin, and drinks to a sanctified ground
under the moonlight sky.
No one worried about bodily harm.
How flying torsos, hips, and legs
easily knock out players.
The wounded were lay
on the cold concrete—prone
green army men.

In the end, the blues and reds
stammered home with bruised
body parts, faint memories
of their day and vivid smiles
of Johnny on the Pony—
swearing at the street-lit darkness
their side had won.

Bogus Realty Company 1

a larry davis story

Prospective clients
get an application.
Agency collects a finder's fee
ninety bucks cash.
Now a client, they're told
to come back.

Mad crazy motherfucker paid his fee.
Back with his sister apartment-less
quoting the fine print;
requesting a refund.

Secretary with a half attitude
points to the manager.
This was just a summer job, hook up.
Her sister's godmother
is screwing the owner.

A silver gun flash
inside the storefront.
Shit gets serious.

Secretary calls her mother.
Chums answers the phone Yes, baby?
Secretary to Chums There's a gun on Mr. Keyes belly,
 can I come home?"
Chums to secretary Yes! Right now!
Secretary to Chums with a nervous tone "OK!"

Secretary to Larry Davis:
 I am going home now!
Secretary to Mr. Keyes:
 I quit!
Larry Davis to the secretary:
 Sit the fuck down

bitch!

Secretary starts sobbing—
I want to go home to my mother.
God touches Larry's heart—
her ass takes off.

Weapons Count

a larry davis Story

I know what they
saying 'bout me
I done heard everything!
Predator, Killah, Loco Larry…
Nobody ever said it
to my face
and lived.
I got my first gun from a
dead Porto Rican kid I used
to know—Jimmy Perez;
a Smith and Wesson.
What mugs didn't know is
his momma named 'em Je-sús.
Nothing is brand new around here.
In this place, Stanley don't sell
clean guns from the back of his car.
You got to learn how to recycle.
Best you can hope for is a low count.
My 16 gauge can't be traced.
This .45-cal—four counts.
That .32-cal—one count.
The .357—nothing…yet.

If I die, read it on page
fourteen.
If I don't, you'll see it
on page one.

Operation Condor

a larry davis Story

Larry as a metaphor.
A genocidal war
on Black and Latino men.
A world bigger than
the block.
Five arrests each night swept
us off our feet; perennial
cattle for the prison industrial
com-plex is organized
crime. Does it operate
without the silent agreement of
law enforcement?

Men in blue snort
cocaine off their squad car
dashboards shouting
—you better have my money
or you a dead mug.
Who is a cocaine
baby, arresting crack
babies?
Are baby pockets
not Broad-way
babies, too?

No one is to blame
but the Robin Hood
of the Ghetto.

Some say, they said.
Larry would kill you,
for absolutely
no reason

Not guilty! Sixteen.

How many
times
they gonna
prosecute us?

If their knees are
knocking they are not
going to church to
cry over his body. Fealty
no matter how heinous
the crime, we support our
cops.
How do you—
What it takes to—
            survive,
when an entire
precinct is after
your shadow
and you?

Loco Larry

a larry davis Story

He was no rapper but
his arrests and probationariory record
read like the lyrics of a death row mc.

Turf wars against crack kingpins
left rival bodies brittle, broken, and
at the mercy of the wind.
No one cared on 43rd street
as our lives were being tuned out
to the sounds of Bruce's Hornsby's,
The Way It Is.

NYPD E.S.U. did not hold hands
with suspects. It did not stroll
a week before Thanksgiving and
offered you cranberry sauce.
They descended like Gabriel and
Michael, swords in one hand
and lady justice on the other,
ready to offer last rights.

Not until Officer Buckley lost her face,
did the typewriters stop.
A new clean 20-pound sheet of paper
rolled and clung to the drum
like backyard laundry on any afternoon
on Staten Island.
      It was a mess.
      Her lost face.
How could we not let our hearts pour out?
Both straight and stray bullets made her
a more detached killer when she returned
to duty as a police sniper.

Larry escaped through an unguarded

window. The boroughs, always on the alert.
Another black man hunted through
concrete marshes, and brick forests
Not sure if it was all myth or bio-epic movie.
Our lives have always had part-time value.
Desperate and Fox, he was,
crawled for refuge into the projects.
Took a mother and her two children
hostage--negotiated a coward's surrender.

Social justice mobsters sucker-punch cops
in New York while the peaceniks cheered.
After his death, the mayor said he was a killer.
He shot six cops. That we should not
take pride in the execution of anybody--
illegally. But he believed that there was
a special oil pot in hell for him.

Larry Davis used children
as human shields.
Hell yeah, he did.

Bogus Realty Company 2

a larry davis Story

That motherfucker shot 20 cops.
I was jumping up and down screaming
that's him, that's him.

I dream about that day a lot.
Of picking up the phone
and calling Chums
instead of the police.
He couldn't believe it.

I guess he was just shocked
that I could be so brazen
or maybe God touched his heart.

My mother did call the police,
and he did rob Mr. Keyes.
Not only for the fee but
for the day's take.

I don't have any sympathy for that fucker.
I was eighteen,
and he could have killed me.

Charges

a larry davis Story

They came to arrest
him, to bring a son
to justice. Bullets pierce
through walls, blood seeped
into parquet.
Republicans and Democrats
wore red and blue blazers.
Cheered the six
o'clock news like Yankees
and Red Sox fans.
The blind lady tipped
the scale and charges
multiplied.

Bonfire of the Vanities

a larry davis Story

They call them material
witnesses, specs of dust
and oil residue; evidence.

Research professionals offer
testimony, lead investigators
gather them all.

This is not Broadway
but line by line meticulously
they pause at every coma.

Teams of wardrobe and jury
consultants work to bring life
to bent backs and knees.

They enter these halls
of justice prepared to fight
for their version of the truth.

In its magnetic code
a surreptitious tape
carries another account.

Although justice might be
blindfolded, sooner or later
its gavel will strike.

Robo Cop

a larry davis Story

What is it like! We have a saying
around the precinct, you know.

"Nineteen years in the South Bronx beat
hardens a man, even a Catholic priest."

Don't write that. But it is pretty funny.
If you have seen the things, I've seen…

I don't drink before work. It slows
down my reflexes and when you deal

with pieces of shit like Larry Davis,
you got to be ready. Kill or be Kill.

Is that fucking simple! These animals
don't care. They are ready to eat his bones.

Feel! I don't feel shit. I've been desensitized
to this shit hole since my rookie year.

The Mayor doesn't care. These Landlord bastards
burn people out to collect insurance money.

What's my stake? I live in fucking long Island.
You think I want to drive here to get killed.

Fuck you! We all toil in these sewers.
I just want to make it home every night.

I hate everything about this place.
They don't appreciate the work that I do.

I haven't survived for 20 years because
I care, nope. Whatever it takes, man.

Look at me! My knee, my hand, my thigh
I'm fucking RoboCop now and for what.

So these animals can let him go free.
Let me tell you something, everyone!

And I mean—every-one wanted him dead;
no one—wanted the paperwork.

Yes, Lord

a larry davis Story

Only mothers understand what
kind of grief brews inside a
womb. The same womb that
nurtured and cared for him.

It is umbilical, primordial, and
physical in memory, how it keeps her
company. She is not a widow, but
she does sleepwalk.

There was comfort in small
words when the verdict came
down. Sixteen times not
guilty. Grief whispered:Hallelujah.

People in the gallery talk about
Black people no longer being
Sambos but Black Rambos.

A mother knows grief and
it will soon return.

Thursday 7:00 PM

a larry davis story

Stabbed repeatedly in his
arms, head, back, legs, and
chest.

At the hands of another
badass inmate wielding a
nine-inch shank.

Fell in the yard of an upstate
prison, and thereupon hangs
the strange tale

of Larry Davis my linebacker/
quarterback; notorious killer and
antihero of my youth.

El South Bronx

Has the largest population of Puerto Rican colonial subjects outside of the colony that is Puerto Rico.

The Moor of The Bronx

I return to what has always been a gated community, surrounded by graffiti and its low art understory – a beastly conversation – and a swarm of pigeons bombarding the streets with their Manta-Ray shadow – no one worries about the sky falling – the wind makes nothing out of feces. I stand here where the trees look older and meager like the people who are familiar to them.

Few are the things that bear fruit, Pagodas, Magnolias, and Sassafras. Someone dried the willow groves – a symbol of my absence. I have come home 200 feet above sea level. I have never tasted the salt in the wind – each memory I hold is stale with faceless cutouts of people who were friends – this is hallowed ground – as life's legend proclaims – each generation shedding its skin for the next. Many measured their time by the art on the wall, how one generation ignores the other, yet another protects the next.

I return to the memories of blood dried on red brick walls, to missing memorials for bullets kissed with my name – where a simple push guaranteed a life – This is my Boogie Down, The Bronx of further over there – a place absent of tornados, where bodies swell if not for the thousands of witnesses who always hear something but never see anything – I stand here, ready to unbury what we all have never forgotten, waiting for another push – for I was guaranteed by a life unmarked and flesh that lays imbedded in brick layered walls.

The Crease of Almidón

I am from forgotten bodies in fingerprinted chairs and gurneys.
From kidnapped bullets screaming for salvation.
From broken limbs and shattered skulls that won't be home tonight.

I am from bedrooms too small for two or more brothers.
From folding cots and leaned mattresses that disappear at sunrise.
From nails too old and wood too brittle to hold up the sky.

I am from transformed living rooms that double as Ellis Island.
From bathroom lines that form and begin with four boys and three girls.
From go get dressed while your brothers and sisters eat.

I am from *almidón* and perfectly creased shirts and trousers.
From thermal underwear, and you can't go outside without a T-shirt.
From repaired knees, a clean kitchen, and always the smell of King Pine.

I am from *avena, pan con queso, and café con galletas cada tres horas.*
From *dulce de papaya, pasta de guayaba y todo lo que causa diabetis.*
From *chicharrones, ñanicletas y todas las frituras que dan alta presión.*

I am from *hice poquito but llevale este plato a Iris.*
From have you eaten is the follow-up question to hello.
From you always look pale and *flaco* and *tomate una malta.*
I am from *mil abrazos y besos* in the company of *pésame* tears.
From *hay Dios mio, dejame verte y date la vuerta.*
From all that is true and false about people in red brick buildings.

I am from the womb of women with extra-large hearts.

Angels on the Corner

The Bronx, midnight twenty-three minutes past. She comes to me for the first time since my return. To where the cobblestones lay and the trolley's echoes are but a long-forgotten ghost. I stood on the corner that doubled as a bus stop—where thirty-three years earlier, he stood against the doorway, a man Black, quiet and invisible to how many others besides me.
I hear him tonight; mature in his voice, teaching me how to survive. "Do you see a Taxi sign?" "You know he doesn't have to stop once you get in." He says to me, again. My hand released the handle and I stepped back on the curb like a would-be slaughtered animal. Fear rushed through my body like a caravan of rats. The number two and one arrive at the same time—I look back and nod—he engraves me. I shuffle into the bus, with this secret clenched in my hand and the image of his voice: an angel. Her car pulls to the curb—this time, I know whose handle I am holding.

Annabel Lee and Me

Corner after corner, the Bronx reveals itself to me—in grey morning dew, throughout sleepy worship afternoons. Under tenement shadow, blackbirds linger in the sky, waiting for dark berries to stain the ground. I sat on the corner of Poe Park, to imagine the cottage when there was nothing but grass. I push everything out of my head, the bicycles, the unremitting sirens, and the sound that air makes when buses brake. I try to travel in time, to let this place rush up, as it used to be before my people were forged. I am intimate with the lay of this land. My hands rise and fall across its stomach, and I make casts of its hills. A thrill of wind races up my spine, and I consider this feeling of being on my own again. The brood that used to pool inside me gives over to elation; the relief is remarkable.

Autumn in the Bronx

Yellow brick stands next to chalky chocolate tenements.
Cobblestone lays quiet under asphalt blankets.
Teenage ghosts play like children at sleepovers.

A slate-gray mist falls against the dusk. Somewhere
on Gun Hill Road, Carl will die. We will not learn
about it until the dampened thud of fifty bound
newspapers mimic him.

Nighttime undresses behind the crisp rattle of gates.
Soda cans rumble in the breeze like orphans.
The wind begins to stir. I inhale the moisture in the air.
I think about whose name I will read in the paper.

Tap Out

for Wild Moreno and all the Bronx Boppers

"The Rain is over, the flood is dry, why do you wear your pants so high?" " While the flood was here, my pants got wet, The higher I wear them the dryer they get!" South Bronx snap

We were cool
Rapping and Snapping
Que Pasa! My Brothers and Sisters.
Back in 69 on Morris Ave
We remember the names of those
who rest in peace.
Let's give props to them,
Those pretty cool, fun-loving kids,
living wild in a world of shit.
I tap out some of my beer to the dead
even today tambien, I do not forget
where I came from.
This wild kid made it out,
but not without suffering
Keep it real with a feel!
You—who stayed back
and lived.

The Other Side of Plexiglas

Pútos be on the street throwing rocks
acting bad like Fuck You mister cock-sucking cop.
Maricón, I fuck you up the ass like American Me.
Talking shit on the other side of Plexiglas shields
to that motherfucker from middle school. The one
they used to give a wedgie to.

He grew up fast, lost himself in the back of comic books,
swearing no fucking jock was ever going to kick sand
in his mother's fucking face. Got an A in Gym, a job
cleaning the weight lifting room, a key to the wrestling ring,
where he got pinned every time but never stayed down.

This motherfucker

Never forgot the scraping of metal against
his teeth' enamel made his lips swell.
How laughter cemented to his body
when he fell to the ground at lunchtime.
He blamed his parents for his genetics,
his lousy nutrition and terrible social condition,
every time.

When he became a cop,
he swore upon a rosary every day
that things would not fall apart.
The way he felt his family, teachers, and principals
let him hurt on the inside of a locker, a laundry basket
or the perennial fall down marble stairs. He always gave up
his sit and lunch, each week, each day, at the noon hour.
So when *Putos* be Fuck You
on the other side of Plexiglas,
he is taking notes for the next time he sees you,
he is gonna pay it all back
in kind.

Window Washers

With the eyes of a raven, single mothers
like window washers perched in the sky
tracked the shadows of birds of prey.
These widows, abandoned at conception,
sometimes once and twice, lived with men
made of tamarind bark. Not exotic, rough
and sour but sweet when the right time
of the year arrived.
Pañuelo signals undulate like *banderas*
at the Puerto Rican Day Parade

>   *Ahi va ese, velalo!*
>   *Que te ejta mirando la nena!*

And we watched them *como en velorios.*
Nueve rosarios en nueve noches
these *muertos* retreating into the shadows.
En Guerra they prayed against *el Diablo.*
They never gave up on us
los que salimos de su vientre.
Madres hoy en el cielo our streets
blindsided by unearthed predators.

No Obituary

He didn't die on the subway platform
where he was stabbed from the back
by an unknown face.
He clung to every breath and step,
walked through the concourse exit
of the independent D train line,
468 steps from his mother's door.

It had rained the day before, and
he channeled his way across the
boulevard, between cars, stumbling
against Alfon's 1979 grey TransAM.
His his fingerprint, already dried
by the next morning, smeared
on the driver's side fender.

His blood, crimson as the color
of bricks, traced a trail of his DNA
back to the crime scene.
Breathing the air held more secrets.
Soft hearts, hardened
in the early morning darkness.

Safe en Casa

for Maylin Reynoso and all the missing Bronx girls

Maybe it was the silence que *borró*
tus feelings at thirteen because
no hija mia va a salir preña.

A lo mejor it was *polque una noche*
te fuiste anyway *y regresaste creyendo*
que aparentemente habias crecido.

Perhaps it was how you tried to vomit
in the middle of the night quiet,
pensando que estavamos dormidos.

Quizás you forgot *que las*
paredes eran de carton, y death
se levantava inside of you.

Probably when we notice que *tu*
no estabas, no one believed us.
Era como si el silent game *te borró.*

¿A donde fuiste, a la casa del novio
que no tenias y nadie conocía?
Donde te abrieron las piernas

and your tears and your blood
se mezclaban en fiero terror.
Your voice *como buche ultrajada.*

Abuelas muertas didn't say *¡Ay bandito!*
Machetes in anger were not pulled
from homemade newspaper shifts.

No one cursed God.
No se encontró justicia.
Nadie se asomó.

When the periódico *publico tu retrato,*
You were wearing a blue plaid skirt
and a white blouse. *Pocos se acordaban*

si el uniforme de SacradeHeart *estaba*
supuesto a protejerte from all predators,
including those closest to you, family.

Hambre

My first government meal
came out of a tin colored can
marked "beef" by blocked letters
and a silhouette of a black cow.
Lo estaban repartiendo mom said,
she got on the line to get one.

This was Puerto Rico,
in the early 1970s
before the steel and lead burned
her flesh; we ran under the cover
of night, the hum of transformers
silenced the panic in our steps.
Scattered by her words, *corran.*
She thought he, who
was not our father
went for the *revolver.*
Forgetting that in the future,
when three bullets made of copper
pierced his leg, intestine and chest,
she would nurse him.

On my knees
next to the refrigerator
on the floor
I opened the not yet rusted can
and exclaimed *tiene moco!*
I was a wise four or five
when she explained gelatin
as a thickening agent.
Reassured again.
Walked on broken glass
imitating a yogi I once saw.
Cut open my foot
and she convinced me
I would not bleed out.

My next government meal
came from a doorway
of an abandoned building
at 1065 Gerard Avenue.
This was long before
the construction renaissance
gave life back to a rectangular block
of ten tenements no longer suited
for the living.
This was the summer of 1979
in the South Bronx.

We ran that night--all the way back.
Behind, we left the collective pain
of mountain living, kisses warm as
asphalt. Girls too young to bear love
in the lemongrass. India my first love,
the tamarind tree,and the addiction
to a man of violence.

Poverty was an old husband
with a new job he could not
keep. In this the South Bronx
The country of my birth
husbands and wives
forsake one another
for one extra meal.

*Si le dicej que tu marido te abandonó
el* welfare also spelled farewell,
*te dan 150 pesos mas. Ay chica
no seas sangana, si eso lo hace
to el mundo.*

So, we abandoned his name
and renounced his metal rights
to the family.
We relegated him
to a title not earned.

El Building

Puerto Ricans loved a good migration,
usually at midnight,
three days before rent was due,
mattresses undulating like flags
cast shadows under street lamps.
We were always moving
from a basement dwelling
to a 5th floor walkup with a view.
It was a real-life motherfucking
Jefferson's story, moving on up
at 115 McClellan Street.
The only tenement that had a photo studio,
purse factory, chicken farm, bbq pit,
party hall, basketball court, volleyball net
and a dog kennel all under one roof.

La Yarda!

La Yarda, doubled as a firework launching pad,
on random, *esto no es el* South Bronx holidays.
Like, kill the rat day, *sacaron la basura* day,
barrieron el basement day, *mapiaron las escalera* day,
deja de estal escribiendo en la pared day, *tiene limbe de coco* day,
and *comprame una fria* day.

Even after confirmation to the Supreme Court, we
have always been the children of migrants.
Long after the Siwanoy exodus of survival,
the British and Dutch molten iron that created
Van Cortlandt's forgotten mass graves.
The Jewish Grand Concourse,
a promenade of faded nostalgia tours
abandoned along with the community's Easter parade.

If They See Us

Telling the truth
was a lie.
Survival meant
what lie
could we tell
that they
would believe?
In the interrogation room,
at fourteen,
they forced us
to want their women.
Our secret,
that we liked
Jo, Molly, and Blair
was a sunrise
after a squall.
This haunting
was for the first
not the guilty.

We swelled!

While we were wilin' out
they heard wildin',
tried to decipher
cultural references
requiring more than
philistine conversations.
No longer innocent,
pure and precious,
our childhood burst
long after
the tobacco fields
of our grandparents.
This inheritance;
a genetic disease of our
hemoglobin. A blood

and bone marrow
cure for the few.

We swelled!

In our hands
and feet; fatigued
during the chase,
tired marathoners
des sables.
During the accusation.
abdominal pains
from hunger;
long since the migration
north, across Harlem
in pursuit of comfort
Since 1889
undocumented
tellings' of us
bowed heads
scared them
and our feet, bare,
blistered in the fire.

Concentric Days

Last summer outing:
People trickle out of the subway like rain. The air sweats.
His chest thumps, waiting for the corpse flower to bloom.
Too many holiday weekend hats look the same.

5:59 A.M.
He stands in autumn—quiet is the rustle of leaves
that drag the wind along the road. They settle at his feet.
Streetlights imitate yellow sac spiders.

Scarecrow tonight:
He turns from where the sun will rise; the search remains.
His reckoning will not be accurate. Nervous hands dab
inside his pockets. He feels the texture of his fingerprints.

Winter Solstice:
First frost this year; fingers uncoil and curl inside
the leather jacket. What kind of trees were these
when they had leaves? He notices their fragile look.

A random day in February:
The corner trash can overflows. A crushed beer can
plays hopscotch across the street. There are no birds
perched on the power lines.

First week in March:
A musketeer keeps a sword by his side. The thumb,
ready to press the release button. The springs,
new and strong. It hasn't rained yet.

May:
Nature's price is paid through thorns. Where do
domestic flowers grow? There's a calmness to blood.
There aren't enough petals to await her return.

Fuego

> "After years of fire experience, fire prevention, and fire investigation, I feel that...rather than being accidental, fire is largely a social problem and the Bronx has and will have its share of such problems." NYC Deputy Fire Chief Charles Kirby, March 1970

A handsome young,
Puerto Rican man, freshly cut
goatee and greaser hairstyle,
eyes the color of marbles
lies on a kitchen floor,
unresponsive.
Around him
the Bronx is burning
and no one seems to care.
Like him, the Boogie Down
was hooked on drugs,
and there was not enough ice
and cold water
to revive it.

We entered at our own risk
junkies and pushers
Ignoring spray-painted signs
and bullet-chipped marble.
All that was once grand
about this working class
suburb became split
north and south of I-95.

We played round up
with our lives.
Maletas packed every night;
no agencia had booked a trip to
Isla Verde. When *el grito de fuego*
echoed inside our walls we moved
west from the south but
like roaches, fire followed us.

So, we moved with Tia to a
eso ta caliente neighborhood.
And four to a bunk bed
became a style of living.

Fort Apache, known for the
broken bodies of *tecatos y tecatas i*
inside basement clubhouses
painted in black—highlighted in neon,
became our Little House
on the Prairie.

Lost to the decade;
62 out of 94 thousand residents.
Herman Ridder Junior High
with its Cupola casting shadows
could not save 6 out of 10 students.
The only building on the block
that had not been abandoned,
burned by arson, or both,
we all fled.

Papo Hueso

I was born in the South Bronx, where *manteca*
skied in the *venas of tecatos. Donde cuerpos*
lay stiff like green army men.

On the morning of my birth, Miguelito,
the local junky was found *jeringuilla* hanging
from his vein; half sitting at the kitchen table
of his tenement basement apartment.

Just about every Puerto Rican in the block- Juan,
Miguel, Milagros, Olga y Manuel- worked in some
lame ass garment district job; barely making enough
for a *Mortadella con queso* sandwich.

Marisol La Loca—well she wasn't *crazy* crazy but
for the right price, she would let you watch Benji
the dog fuck her. People said she was *tostada,*
but what she was *–era una deseperarción* to feed
an *heroina* habit, which made her do *loca* things.

Papo Hueso, one of her tricks
who didn't care if he came first or second
to Benji *decía,* hey, the dog is a client, too.
He was always running cold and often
envied *la lengua del perro.*

On the afternoon of my scheduled arrival
Puntilla, the building, super *descubrió* a Benji
humping Marisol's dead body. She had been
stabbed, and her ears were missing.

La gente, hanging out of opened back yard windows
like a Westside story *gritaban, eso fue el perro.* Benji—
who was fluent in broken Spanish, Poodle, Pincher
and occasional stray cat dialects—understood enough
to know *perro* was in trouble.

By the time people began to pay attention
to him, he was leading detectives on a chase
out of the apartment, up to the rooftop and down
a rusted fire escape ladder to *Papo Hueso's* third floor
bedroom. There three *policías* watched him eat
a *plato of arroz con sangre.*

I was twelve pounds on the night I was born; both
my mother and I had our eyes open.

Dr. Ricardo Nazario-Colón is an accomplished Higher Education Administrator with over twenty years of experience in various industries, including the U.S. Military, Colleges & Universities, Corporate Banking, and State Government. He is the inaugural Chief Diversity Officer and Inclusive Executive at Western Carolina University. He also serves as President of the Appalachian Studies Association, 2022-23. He was the former Chair of the University of North Carolina System Diversity and Inclusion Council and the Governor's Advisory Council on Hispanic Latino Affairs.

He is a published poet with numerous publications in journals and anthologies and has authored two poetic books *Of Jíbaros and Hillbillies*, Plain View Press 2011 and *The Recital*, Winged City Press 2011. His forthcoming book under contract is *Latinx Voices in Appalachia*, University Press of Kentucky, 2024. His research focuses on Black culture centers, multiracial identity experience, student leadership development, and African American faculty and staff retention.

He is a former U.S. Marine, a Life member of Phi Beta Sigma Fraternity, Inc., and a co-founder of the Affrilachian Poets. He earned a Doctorate in Higher Education Leadership from Western Carolina University, a Masters in Secondary Education from Pace University, and a Bachelors in Spanish Literature and Latin American Studies from the University of Kentucky.

www.ingramcontent.com/pod-product-compliance
Lightning Source LLC
Chambersburg PA
CBHW031126160426
43192CB00008B/1128